Helping Children See Jesus

ISBN: 978-1-64104-019-8

Service
New Testament Volume 18: Acts Part 5

Author: Ruth B. Greiner
Illustrator: Frances H. Hertzler
Colorization courtesy of Good Life Ministries
Typesetting and Layout: Morgan Melton, Patricia Pope

© 2018 Bible Visuals International
PO Box 153, Akron, PA 17501-0153
Phone: (717) 859-1131
www.biblevisuals.org

All rights reserved. No part of this publication may be reproduced, stored in a retrieval system or transmitted in any form by any means, electronic, mechanical, photocopy, recording or otherwise, without the prior permission of the publisher, except as provided by USA copyright law.

RELATED ITEMS

To access related items (such as activities, memory verse posters and translated texts) please visit our web store at shop.biblevisuals.org and enter 1018 in the search box on the page.

FREE TEXT DOWNLOAD

To access a FREE printable copy of the teaching text (PDF format) in English or other available languages, enter S1018DL in the search box. Add the item to your cart, and use coupon code XTACSV17 at checkout. Once your order is processed you will receive an email with a link to the free download.

I beseech you therefore, brethren, by the mercies of God, that ye present your bodies a living sacrifice, holy, acceptable unto God, which is your reasonable service.

Romans 12:1

Lesson 1
PAUL'S FIRST MISSIONARY JOURNEY

NOTE TO THE TEACHER

The lessons in this volume trace the missionary journeys of Paul. Is there any value in learning distances between cities? Is something to be gained by memorizing the geography of Paul's travels? It is far more important that each student learn (1) the distance that separates a human heart from God; (2) the importance of bringing his wandering heart to the Saviour; (3) the privilege it is to serve the Lord.

Since your class may want a complete record of the places Paul visited, we have listed them together with numbers. The numbers correspond with those on the map (pages 16 and 17). You may print all the places named or only those mentioned in the lesson itself. If more than one number is given, it is because the missionaries went to those places more than once.

If possible, study the excellent Moody Press paperback titled *The Acts of the Apostles* by Dr. Charles Caldwell Ryrie.

For each of the journeys, your students should list in their notebooks: (1) the reason for the journey; (2) important events of the journey and (3) the results of the journey.

Encourage them to draw a map indicating some of the places named. They may want to illustrate some of the foremost events (using the visuals in this book as a guide).

Every believer has an appointed place of service in the army of the Lord–a spot chosen by God Himself. The situation may be difficult or pleasant. Whichever, it is a place of privilege.

Entering the work of the Lord demands total commitment and dedication to Him. Each must examine himself to see if he is worthy. He must be a blood-bought child of God, cleansed from sin. Places visited on missionary journey #1:

1. (#13) Antioch (in Syria)
2. Salamis (in Cyprus) Cyprus was the home of Barnabas. Paul, Barnabas and John Mark were together.
3. Paphos (Cyprus) Because Elymas tried to keep Sergius Paulus from believing, he was blinded temporarily.
4. (#12) Perga (in Pamphylia) John Mark goes home; Paul feels this is not justified.
5. (#11) Antioch (Pisidia–Province of Galatia–Asia Minor) Paul and Barnabas. Jews refuse Gospel message so missionaries turn to Gentiles; Jews force them to leave.
6. (#10) Iconium Threatened stoning.
7. (#9) Lystra People wanted to offer sacrifices to Paul and Barnabas, who restrained them. Two miracles: (1) lame man healed; (2) Paul raised up (either resurrected or restored) from stoning.
8. Derbe
9. (#7) Lystra
10. (#6) Iconium
11. (#5) Antioch (Pisidia)
12. (#4) Perga
13. (#1) Antioch (Syria)

Scripture to be studied: Acts 9:20-31; 13:1–14:28. Galatians 1:10-24

The *aim* of the lesson: To teach that God wants each believer to serve Him.

> **What your students should *know*:** Giving their lives to God for service is a privilege.
>
> **What your students should *feel*:** A desire to give themselves to the Lord Jesus for His service.
>
> **What your students should *do*:** Obey the Lord by telling the Gospel message.

Lesson outline (for the teacher's and students' notebooks):

1. God protects Paul so he can serve the Lord (Acts 9:23-30; 13:1-4).
2. Paul preaches to Sergius Paulus, a Roman ruler (Acts 13:5-41).
3. The Jewish leaders become jealous of Paul (Acts 13:42–14:5).
4. People respond to the Gospel message in different ways (Acts 14:6-28).

The verse to be memorized:

> *I beseech you therefore, brethren, by the mercies of God, that you present your bodies a living sacrifice, holy, acceptable unto God, which is your reasonable service.* (Romans 12:1)

THE LESSON

To Paul the highest honor was to be a servant of the Most High God. (See Philippians 3:14.) In his letters to the churches he spoke of himself as a servant (a slave, literally) of Jesus Christ. (See Romans 1:1; Philippians 1:1.) He served God for two reasons: (1) The Lord had called him to be a servant; (2) Paul *wanted* to serve God–he served by choice.

There had been a time when Paul *thought* he was serving the Lord God. Instead, he had done the opposite. He had worked *against* God by persecuting Christians. But one day he was converted and became a new man in Christ.

Immediately Paul asked, "Lord, what do You want me to do?" And the Lord answered, "Go into the city, and you will be told what you must do."

Soon Paul understood that God had chosen him to be a messenger of the Lord Jesus Christ. What a responsibility!

Paul had studied the Jewish teachings and received the best education. After his conversion he needed time to think about Christ the Lord. So he went to a solitary place (in the Arabian desert) to study and prepare for the years of service that lay ahead. (See Galatians 1:15-18.)

There in the desert Paul learned many truths. He realized that everyone needed to be saved by believing in the Lord Jesus Christ. He understood that Christian believers all have the same standing in the sight of God. Slaves and masters; rich and poor; yellow, black, white, red and brown; Jews and Gentiles–all who believe in Jesus Christ and receive Him as Lord and Saviour are one. Paul knew that God wanted him to take this news to the world. *How* did he know? We are not certain. But he doubtless prayed some of the prayers of the Psalmist: "Teach me to do Your will; for You are my God . . . lead me" (Psalm 143:10). "Show me Your ways, O Lord; teach me Your paths" (Psalm 25:4). "For Your name's sake lead me, and guide me" (Psalm 31:3b). And it was encouraging to Paul to read this promise of God: "I will instruct you and teach you in the way which you shall go: I will guide you with My eye" (Psalm 32:8).

1. GOD PROTECTS PAUL SO HE CAN SERVE THE LORD
Acts 9:23-30; 13:1-4

After about three years of preparation, Paul was ready to serve Jesus Christ. He was eager to spread the Gospel. He preached first in Damascus, the very place he had once gone to capture and bind all the Christians. But those who hated Christ hated Paul also. So they made plans to take his life.

Show Illustration #1

Paul's Christian friends learned that his enemies were going to kill him. So they went to Paul at night, got him into a basket, and let him down over the city wall. Because God had much more for Paul to do, He helped him escape.

Paul headed for Jerusalem. There he spoke boldly about the Lord Jesus. And the people planned to kill him. (See Acts 9:26-30.) Again he escaped and went to his hometown, Tarsus. Some years before when Paul left Tarsus, he had been a respected Jewish student. Returning, he was despised because he had become a Christian. How difficult it must have been for him during the ten years he stayed there!

Paul was willing to go wherever the Lord sent him. The Lord could help him to escape as before. Or, if He purposed to take Paul to Heaven, Paul was prepared for that.

In the city of Antioch (in Syria–#1 on map) the Holy Spirit called Paul and Barnabas to go together to other lands to spread the good news of salvation. After the Antioch church leaders prayed for them, Paul, Barnabas and a helper, John Mark, stopped first on Cyprus (#2 on map–the former home of Barnabas).

2. PAUL PREACHES TO SERGIUS PAULUS, A ROMAN RULER
Acts 13:5-41

Show Illustration #2

Across the island at Paphos (#3 on map), the Roman ruler (Sergius Paulus) asked Paul and Barnabas to teach him about God. But Elymas, a worker of magic, tried to keep the Roman from trusting the Lord. Paul glared at Elymas and exclaimed, "You son of the devil! You enemy of all true goodness! You are full of trickery and evil! It is time for you to stop opposing the Lord. God is going to punish you. You will be blind for a while."

Instantly Elymas went blind and begged for someone to lead him by the hand.

The Roman ruler was amazed when he saw what happened to Elymas. Immediately he put his trust in the Lord Jesus Christ.

After this the missionaries sailed across the Mediterranean Sea. (See #4.) They were sorry when John Mark decided to return home. Paul and Barnabas, however, went on to the city of Antioch (in Pisidia, a province of Galatia–#5 on map). There, in the synagogue, Paul preached a powerful sermon to the Jews. He reviewed their Jewish history. He told them that the Saviour, Jesus, had died and God had raised Him from the dead. He explained that they could have forgiveness of sins by believing in Him. Then he warned them not to ignore the teaching.

3. THE JEWISH LEADERS BECOME JEALOUS OF PAUL
Acts 13:42–14:5

The news of Paul's preaching spread through the city. When the Gentiles heard about it, they asked Paul to preach to them the next Sabbath (that is, Saturday). This Paul did gladly. And almost all the people in the city heard the Word of God.

Show Illustration #3

The Jewish leaders were jealous because so many listened to Paul. Angrily they spoke against him.

Paul and Barnabas boldly answered: "It was our duty to speak the good news from God to you Jews first. But by rejecting it, you have shown yourselves unworthy of eternal life. So we offer it to the Gentiles."

When the Gentiles heard this they thanked God for His message. And many believed in the Lord Jesus and received His gift of eternal life. This made the Jewish leaders so furious they forced the missionaries out of the city. Do you suppose Paul and Barnabas became discouraged? Were they ready to quit serving God? No! They simply moved on and preached in other cities.

4. PEOPLE RESPOND TO THE GOSPEL MESSAGE IN DIFFERENT WAYS
Acts 14:6-28

At Lystra (#7 on map) many who listened to the missionaries were worshipers of idols. They watched intently when Paul commanded a man who had never walked, "Stand up!" Amazingly, the man stood, leaped and walked!

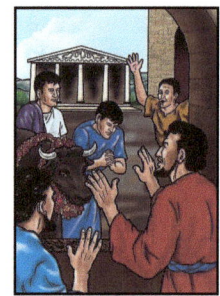

Show Illustration #4

The people were astonished. They shouted, "The gods are come down to us in human bodies!" They called Barnabas by the name of the Greek god, Jupiter; Paul they called Mercury. The priest of the temple brought oxen and garlands of flowers. And the people were ready to offer sacrifices to Paul and Barnabas.

But the two missionaries tore their clothes, shouting, "Why are you doing this? We are human beings like you! We came to urge you to turn from false make-believe gods to the living God. He is the One who made Heaven and earth and sea and everything in them."

Even so, the missionaries could scarcely keep the people from offering their sacrifices. Only a few days later some Jews from other cities (Antioch and Iconium–more than 100 miles away) came. They so stirred up the crowds against Paul that they stoned him, dragged him out of the city and left him for dead.

The very next day Paul and Barnabas were on their way to Derbe (#8 on map) to tell the people there about the Lord Jesus. After revisiting some of the cities to comfort the new believers who were being persecuted, they sailed back to Antioch (in Syria– #13 on map). Their first missionary journey was ended.

They had obeyed the Lord's command to take the Gospel to others. As a result of their obedience, many Jews and Gentiles had been born into the family of God.

Paul and Barnabas gave themselves to the Lord Jesus for His service. Have *you*?

Lesson 2
THE SECOND MISSIONARY JOURNEY

NOTE TO THE TEACHER

As a Christian you–like the Apostle Paul–have a wonderful message to proclaim. You too are a servant of the living God. You are His witness–wherever you are.

The Holy Spirit may not send you to Athens, Ephesus or Corinth. But you are a messenger of the Lord Jesus. Your missionary journey may lead you to people who resent your message. No matter what obstacles you face, continue to serve God. Let your body be a living, holy sacrifice–the kind the Lord can use. When you remember all He has done for you, is this too much to ask?

The missionaries' experiences were almost always the same in every city: they taught the Scriptures in the synagogue; witnessed to individuals and groups; hearers turned to the Saviour; unbelievers opposed them.

Places visited on missionary journey #2:
14. Through Syria Paul and Silas
15. Through Cilicia
16. Derbe
17. Lystra Timothy joins Paul and Silas.
18. Region of Phrygia
19. Galatia Province Here they intended to go to Bithynia but were forbidden by the Holy Spirit.
20. Troas Vision of Macedonian calling for help. Across the Aegean Sea.
21. Neapolis Luke joins the other three.
22. Philippi (Macedonia/Europe) City of first-rate importance in population, prominence, wealth. Lydia, seller of purple cloth, is converted. Demon cast out of girl. Philippian jailer converted. Message: "Believe on the Lord Jesus Christ and thou shalt be saved . . ." Luke may have remained at Philippi.
23. Thessalonica Message: "Jesus is the Christ." Jason (missionaries' host) taken to court.
24. Berea Paul, Silas, Timothy. Opposition to Gospel. Paul is forced to leave.
25. Athens Paul waits for Silas and Timothy to join him. Paul preaches on Mars Hill: "Jesus died and rose. Repent!"
26. Corinth Paul discouraged. Works at his trade–tent-making–with Aquila and Priscilla. Paul preaches: "Jesus is Christ." Mob reaction against him.
27. Ephesus Paul leaves Aquila and Priscilla here.
28. Jerusalem
29. Antioch (home)

Scripture to be studied: Acts 15:36-41; 16:1–18:22

The *aim* of the lesson: To show that no matter how difficult situations are, believers must continue serving God.

What your students should *know*: God wants Christians to serve Him day after day.

What your students should *feel*: A desire to be more faithful in serving the Lord.

What your students should *do*: Make a list of ways they can serve God this week.

Lesson outline (for the teacher's and students' notebooks):
1. Young Timothy joins Paul on his second missionary journey (Acts 16:1-40).
2. Jews at Thessalonica riot against Jason and the Gospel (Acts 17:1-14).
3. Paul preaches to Greeks in Athens and some believe (Acts 17:15-34).
4. The Gospel is preached in Corinth and the Jews refuse to believe (Acts 18:1-2).

The verse to be memorized:

I beseech you therefore, brethren, by the mercies of God, that you present your bodies a living sacrifice, holy, acceptable unto God, which is your reasonable service. (Romans 12:1)

THE LESSON

Paul was ready at all times to serve the Lord. A few years after his first missionary trip he said to Barnabas, "Let's visit each city where we preached to see how the new converts are doing."

Barnabas was eager to go. But others wondered, "Why are you going again? You almost lost your lives on your first journey. Remember how many scorned you and refused to listen to you!"

Paul could answer confidently, "I am not ashamed of the good news about Jesus Christ. It is the power of God to everyone who believes it. I owe it to everyone to tell them about this great salvation."

Barnabas insisted that John Mark should go with them. But because John Mark had left them on the first journey, Paul refused to take him. Paul wanted missionaries who would not turn back. After a sharp argument, Barnabas took John Mark and went to Cyprus. And Paul took an able man, Silas. They went through Syria and Cilicia. (See #14 and #15 on map.) So, instead of one missionary party, there were two!

1. YOUNG TIMOTHY JOINS PAUL ON HIS SECOND MISSIONARY JOURNEY
Acts 16:1-40

Show Illustration #5

At Lystra (#17 on map), Paul and Silas met Timothy, who evidently had been converted the first time Paul visited that city. Timothy's father was a Greek. But his Jewish mother (Eunice) and grandmother (Lois) were believers in Christ. They had taught Timothy the Word of God from the time he was small. (See 2 Timothy 1:5; 3:15.) Timothy loved God and the Scriptures. He was a true example of a believer. Paul, having heard good things about Timothy, decided it would be good to have this young man join them. "Timothy," he said, "would you be willing to travel with Silas and me to witness and teach the Word of God to others?"

If Timothy went, he would miss his family whom he loved. But Timothy loved God most of all. He yearned to be used by Him, and he believed God wanted him to go. "Yes," he answered, "I shall go."

So the three missionaries went together to serve the Lord. They encouraged the Christian believers and led many unbelievers to place their trust in the Lord Jesus. When the missionaries tried to go south (to Asia Minor) and north (to Bithynia), the Holy Spirit forbade them. The specific time for taking the Gospel to those places had not yet come. And these servants of God knew the importance of waiting to be guided by the Spirit of God.

One night while they waited in Troas (#20 on map), Paul had a vision. In the vision a man from Macedonia stood before him and begged: "Come over into Macedonia and help us."

Paul knew then that God wanted him to preach in a new place, Europe. So instead of staying in Asia as he had planned, he sailed across the Aegean Sea. With him were Silas, Timothy and Luke. (See Acts 16:10.)

In Philippi (#22 on map) they had unexpected, wonderful experiences. Lydia, the seller of purple, was converted. A demon was cast out of a young girl. Paul and Silas were thrown into jail. There the two missionaries sang and prayed and witnessed for God. At midnight an earthquake rocked the jail and loosened the prisoners' chains. The jailer and his family turned to God and the missionaries were set free. (*Teacher:* If you did not use NT Volume 17 *Conversion*, tell the events in detail.)

2. THE JEWS AT THESSALONICA RIOT AGAINST JASON AND THE GOSPEL
Acts 17:1-14

Show Illustration #6

In Thessalonica (#23 on map) the missionaries stayed with a man named Jason. He too was a servant of God and served by taking the missionaries into his home.

For three weeks, Paul and Silas went to the synagogue each Sabbath (Saturday). They explained the Scriptures telling that Jesus suffered, died and rose from the dead. Many believed when they heard these wonderful truths.

Others did not believe. In fact some of the religious leaders hated the missionaries' message. So they got a mob of loafers from the streets to start a riot, setting the whole city in an uproar. They attacked Jason's home, planning to drag the missionaries to the rulers of the city. But the missionaries were not there. So they grabbed Jason instead and treated him as a criminal. Why? Because he had let the missionaries stay in his home!

Hauling Jason and some other believers to the city council, the mob shouted, "Paul and his friends have turned the rest of the world upside down! Now they have disturbed our city also! Jason has taken them into his house! They are going against the laws of our emperor, Caesar! They say there is another king called Jesus!"

When the rulers were able to quiet the mob, they made Jason and the other believers promise to send the missionaries away. So the missionaries were sent to the next city along the highway–Berea (#24 on map).

When Paul spoke to the Bereans of Christ, they searched the Scriptures to see if what he said was really true. As a result, many in Berea turned to the Lord. But when the troublesome Jews of Thessalonica heard what was going on, they came and stirred up the Bereans against the missionaries. Once again Paul was forced to escape. Silas and Timothy, however, remained in Berea to encourage the new believers in their faith.

3. PAUL PREACHES TO GREEKS IN ATHENS AND SOME BELIEVE
Acts 17:15-34

In the great city of Athens (#25 on map), Paul walked through the streets. He studied the marble temples and statues of the gods. He was deeply troubled because the people worshiped these lifeless idols.

Day after day Paul went to the synagogue and the marketplace telling about the Lord Jesus. Some men asked, "What does this babbler have to say?" Others answered, "He's telling us about a strange God." They had never heard of the Lord Jesus and His resurrection. Because they were interested in anything new, they brought Paul to Mars Hill, the famous city court of Athens.

Show Illustration #7

There Paul said, "You men of Athens, I see you are very religious. You have images of many different gods. On one altar I saw the words: 'To the Unknown God.' You are worshiping a God you do not know. But I am going to tell you about the true and living God. He is the One who made the world and everything in it. He is the Lord of Heaven and earth. He does not live in temples made with hands. He is too great to be confined to temples. He does not need food or anything you sacrifice to your idols. For *He* is the One who gives life and breath and food to *us*. He is not far from any of us. He wants us to seek Him. *God* is not made of gold or silver or stone. God is not made by *man*. *Man* is made by *God*. And He commands man everywhere to turn to Him repenting of their sin. He will someday judge the world through Jesus whom He raised from the dead."

When Paul spoke about the resurrection of Jesus, some laughed. They thought it was impossible for a person to be raised from the dead. Others said, "We will hear you again about this." But some *did* believe Paul and they put their trust in the living God.

4. THE GOSPEL IS PREACHED IN CORINTH AND THE JEWS REFUSE TO BELIEVE
Acts 18:1-22

After Athens, Paul went to Corinth (#26 on map), a wicked city in Greece. He stayed there for more than one and a half years, living with a Jew named Aquila and his wife, Priscilla.

Show Illustration #8

Aquila and Priscilla were tentmakers. Paul worked with them at their trade. On the Sabbath he went to the synagogue to preach the Gospel–telling about the Lord Jesus Christ, the Son of God.

After Silas and Timothy arrived from Macedonia, Paul spent all his time telling the Jews about Jesus, the One sent by God. They wouldn't believe and said bad things about Jesus. Paul made gestures of brushing off his clothes and announced, "Whatever happens to you is your own doing! From now on I won't give you Jews special treatment but will go with a clear conscience to the Gentiles."

Paul left the synagogue and taught God's Word next door. Crispus, the synagogue leader, his family and many Corinthians placed their trust in the Lord Jesus and were baptized.

Aquila and Priscilla sailed with Paul across the Aegean Sea from Corinth to Ephesus (in Asia Minor, #27 on map). There Paul told the Jews in the synagogue about Jesus Christ. Although he himself could stay only a short time, he left Aquila and Priscilla there with the believers. Then Paul crossed the Mediterranean Sea to Caesarea (Judea). After visiting Jerusalem (#28 on map) he went back to Antioch (#29 on map), and told what God had done on this, his second missionary journey.

Paul's work was not finished. Even though the way had been rough, he was not a quitter. He served God continually. What about *you*? Are you serving Him wherever you are? List in your notebook right now how you can serve God this very week.

Lesson 3
PAUL'S THIRD MISSIONARY JOURNEY

NOTE TO THE TEACHER

The Apostle Paul gave himself to the service of God. He witnessed boldly, not fearing suffering, persecution, nor death. The Lord was with him through his troubles. No one could kill him until his work was done. Teacher, if you are in the will of God, nothing can touch you but that which He allows. Walk fearlessly with Him. Places visited on missionary journey #3:

30. **Ephesus** (Greatest commercial center in Asia at that time) Paul and Luke. Paul healed the sick. Christians burned their magic books. The silversmiths led a riot, "Great is Diana of the Ephesians!"
31. Macedonia
32. Achaia (Greece)
33. Corinth
34. Macedonia
35. Philippi
36. **Troas** Eutychus slept; fell out of window; Paul lifted him up; his life returned.
37. Assos
38. **Miletus** Ephesian elders came to meet with Paul. Last farewell.
39. **Tyre** (Phoenicia) Paul warned not to go to Jerusalem.
40. Ptolemais
41. **Caesarea** Paul stayed with Philip the evangelist. Agabus prophesied that Paul would be bound in Jerusalem.
42. **Jerusalem** Paul imprisoned.

Scripture to be studied: Acts 18:23–21:40

The *aim* of the lesson: To teach that the Lord God plans all that happens to believers who are walking in His will.

What your students should *know*: God wants all believers to give their lives to Him.

What your students should *feel*: A desire to be a bold witness for the Lord.

What your students should *do*: Allow the Lord to lead and use them in witnessing this week.

Lesson outline (for the teacher's and students' notebooks):
1. Paul preaches in Ephesus and many give up their magic (Acts 18:24–19:22).
2. Ephesian silversmiths riot against the Gospel message (Acts 19:23–20:2).
3. A young man in Troas falls to his death and is restored to life (Acts 20:6-12).
4. Paul goes to Jerusalem and is imprisoned (Acts 20:14–21:40).

The verse to be memorized:

I beseech you therefore, brethren, by the mercies of God, that you present your bodies a living sacrifice, holy, acceptable unto God, which is your reasonable service. (Romans 12:1)

THE LESSON

Paul had promised the people of Ephesus: "I shall come again if it is the will of God." It *was* God's will, and Paul did return to Ephesus (#30 on map).

Persecutions and all the enemies of Christ could not stop Paul from going on his third missionary journey. He left from Antioch, as he had done on his first two journeys, not knowing what was ahead of him. He spoke encouraging words to new believers on his way to Ephesus.

1. PAUL PREACHES IN EPHESUS AND MANY GIVE UP THEIR MAGIC
Acts 18:24–19:22

In Ephesus, the famous commercial city, Aquila and Priscilla welcomed Paul. They had been working diligently for the Lord since he left them and they had much to tell him. This time Paul would not rush away, for he had come to stay a while.

For three months Paul preached about Jesus in the Ephesus synagogue. But many Jews refused to believe him and spoke openly against the way of Christ.

So Paul left the synagogue and went to a school which was open to him. There, each day for two years, he taught the Word of God to Jews and Greeks. And every person in that district of Asia heard the Gospel! It had not been God's will for Paul to go to Asia on his second missionary journey. But this time God sent Paul and kept him there long enough for the whole area to hear about Jesus.

Paul's preaching was powerful. God also gave him power to do miracles. Sick people were healed. Evil spirits were cast out. The people in Ephesus watched Paul with amazement.

At that time in the city there were seven sons of Sceva, a Jewish priest. They wandered from town to town claiming they could cast out demons. They saw great miracles when Paul used the name of the Lord Jesus Christ. So when these seven saw a man possessed with a demon, they commanded, "By the name of Jesus whom Paul preaches, come out of this man."

The demon inside the man answered, "I know Jesus and I know Paul; but who are you?" Then, instead of coming out of the man, the evil spirit caused the man to leap upon the brothers, one after the other. He threw them down and beat them, tearing off their clothing. Finally the men broke away and ran out of the house naked and wounded.

Word of what happened spread throughout Ephesus. And the name of the Lord Jesus was greatly honored.

Show Illustration #9

At this time the Christians came to understand it was wrong to practice magic. Many in Ephesus confessed their sin, brought their costly magic books (scrolls) and burned them publicly.

2. EPHESIAN SILVERSMITHS RIOT AGAINST THE GOSPEL MESSAGE
Acts 19:23–20:2

After they gave up their practice of magic, the Word of the Lord spread and God multiplied His work. But Satan, the enemy of God, was also at work. In Ephesus there stood a magnificent idol temple–one of the greatest temples in the world at that time. This rich temple had 117 columns of white marble. Each column was the gift of a king. Inside the temple was an image of the goddess Diana. The people believed Diana had fallen from Heaven. Visitors from other lands came to worship this goddess. Many purchased little silver images of Diana enclosed in miniature temples. Demetrius was one of the silversmiths who earned much money making these images. The Ephesians who placed their trust in the Lord Jesus stopped buying images. This distressed Demetrius.

Show Illustration #10

So Demetrius called all the silversmiths together. "Men," he said, "you know we earn our living by making these images. But now in Ephesus and throughout all Asia, this Paul has turned away many people. So we are in danger of losing our business. And the temple of the great goddess Diana–whom Asia and all the world worship–could be destroyed."

When the men heard what Demetrius said, they shouted, "Great is Diana of the Ephesians!" Others joined, causing wild confusion in the city. For two hours the people screamed, "Great is Diana of the Ephesians!"

When the people finally grew tired, the city clerk tried to reason with them. Though the confusion ended and all seemed peaceful, there was no real peace within the hearts of the idol worshipers. Without the living God, there can be no peace.

Paul taught in Ephesus for three years. Then he called the Christians together. After a long, encouraging talk he said goodbye and left the famous city.

3. A YOUNG MAN IN TROAS FALLS TO HIS DEATH AND IS RESTORED TO LIFE
Acts 20:6-12

In Troas (#36 on map) Paul met with the disciples on Sunday, the first day of the week. Many of the believers were doubtless slaves and may have worked all day. But they gathered in the evening to remember Jesus by having the Lord's Supper together. They were eager also to hear the visiting missionary. Paul had so much to tell them, he preached until midnight!

Show Illustration #11

Because the room was crowded, one young man, Eutychus, sat on the sill of an open window. About midnight he fell asleep and dropped from the third floor to the ground below. Paul and some of the other men ran down to Eutychus but he was already dead. Paul threw himself on the young man and put his arms around him. Shortly he declared, "Do not worry! He is alive again!" The people could hardly believe what they heard. But when they saw Eutychus move, they knew it was true. Eutychus was alive and well! The people were amazed at the great power God had given to Paul to bring a man back to life. They went upstairs again and talked and talked–until daylight!

4. PAUL GOES TO JERUSALEM AND IS IMPRISONED
Acts 20:14–21:40

Paul and some Christian friends then sailed from Assos (#37 on map) southward on the Aegean Sea. After stopping at several little islands, they finally arrived at Miletus (#38 on map).

The elders of the Ephesus church came to Miletus to meet the missionaries. Paul told them: "I am going to Jerusalem. I do not know what will happen to me there. The Holy Spirit has told me that I shall have trouble in city after city. That will not hinder me, for I do not count my life dear to myself. I want to finish my work with joy and tell the good news about Jesus Christ. I know I shall not see you again. But do all I have told you during the last three years. (See Acts 20:31.) I have warned you day and night with many tears. And now, brothers, I commit you to God's care."

After he finished speaking, Paul knelt and prayed for them. And they all wept because they would not see him again on earth. Together they walked to the ship and said a tearful goodbye.

When Paul arrived in Caesarea (#41 on map) he was invited to stay in the home of Philip the evangelist. While there, Agabus a prophet arrived from Judea. He took Paul's belt from him. Tying his own hands and feet with it, he said, "This is what the Holy Spirit says will happen: 'The one who owns this belt will be tied up like this by the Jews in Jerusalem. And they will hand him over to the Gentiles.' "

The other believers begged Paul not to go to Jerusalem. But Paul answered, "What do you mean by crying like this and breaking my heart? I am ready not only to be tied up, but also to die at Jerusalem for the name of the Lord."

Finally they stopped pleading and said, "The will of the Lord be done."

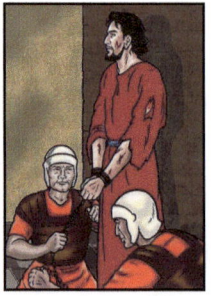

Show Illustration #12

Paul went to Jerusalem (#42 on map) where he was welcomed by the believers. His third missionary journey had ended. But it was not long before he was arrested and thrown into jail as the prophet Agabus had said. Many times God had enabled Paul to escape from his enemies. This time, however, escape was not God's will. But Paul was neither troubled nor discouraged.

He was glad to be a prisoner for the sake of Jesus Christ.

Although Paul's third missionary journey was ended, God had more work for him to do. As a prisoner, he was brought before kings and governors to whom he witnessed boldly. Paul was never ashamed of the Lord, nor was he afraid. He had given his body as a living sacrifice. God was well pleased with His faithful servant, and the rewards which awaited Paul in Heaven far outweighed all the sufferings he endured on earth.

What about you? Have you given yourself as a living sacrifice completely to God? And are you witnessing boldly for Him? God is calling you right now to follow Him. Will you list in your notebook the names of people who this week will hear of the Lord from your lips?

Lesson 4
SERVICE

NOTE TO THE TEACHER

Review the preceding lessons carefully. Show the illustrations and have your students tell the important events of the three missionary journeys.

Emphasize the message the missionaries preached. Make certain your group can state the Gospel clearly:

1. The Lord Jesus Christ is the Son of God.
2. Christ died taking the punishment for our sins.
3. Christ arose from the dead.
4. God forgives the sinner who trusts in Jesus Christ.

At the conclusion of this fourth lesson, help each student to know how to witness personally. A valuable aid for witnessing is a Wordless Book–either ready-made or made by hand. The little book has four pages colored like those on the outside back cover of this volume. The cover should be green. Green is a reminder of grass and trees–growing because they have life.

Scripture to be studied: The verses mentioned in the lesson.

The *aim* of the lesson: To show what God requires of those who would serve Him.

What your students should *know*: God wants them to witness for Him.

What your students should *feel*: A desire to be a witness for the Lord.

What your students should *do*: Present their bodies to God for His service. Plan to tell someone about the Lord Jesus Christ this week.

Lesson outline (for the teacher's and students' notebooks):

1. Anyone who believes in the Lord Jesus can serve God.
2. A servant of God must be yielded to God.
3. God wants His servants to be prepared and trained.
4. True service for God begins now.

The verse to be memorized:

I beseech you therefore, brethren, by the mercies of God, that you present your bodies a living sacrifice, holy, acceptable unto God, which is your reasonable service. (Romans 12:1)

THE LESSON

There are many, many people in the world who have not yet heard the Gospel. God does not want them to be separated from Him forever. (See Matthew 18:14; 2 Peter 3:9.) It is His will that everyone everywhere should trust in His Son, the Lord Jesus Christ. Then, when life is over, believers will be with Him in His home forever. He could send angels to tell the message of salvation. Instead, He wants to use *you* to tell the good news.

God could take you to Heaven the moment you receive His Son as Saviour. Instead He lets you remain on earth to carry His message to the lost around you. He delights to use young people, like Timothy. Timothy gave up the comforts of a loving home to travel as a helper to the older missionaries. Later he became a pastor. God loves to use professional men (like Doctor Luke who traveled with the missionaries). The Lord used Luke's medical ability to heal many who heard the Gospel message from Paul. God also uses men like Jason, who opened his home to the missionaries when they came to his city. And like the missionaries, Jason suffered for his service. God chose certain men–such as Silas and Barnabas–to be effective witnesses, though they are not thought of as great men. And, in His wisdom, God uses others, as He did Paul, to herald His news so effectively that they will be remembered forever.

1. ANYONE WHO BELIEVES IN THE LORD JESUS CAN SERVE GOD

Show Illustration #13

Everyone who comes into this world is a sinner. Because we are sinners, we sin. Very early in life we have sinful habits which cannot be broken. It is as if the sin were tied to our hearts by strong ropes. One alone can free us from sin: the Lord Jesus Christ. When He died on the cross, He took on Himself all our sins. When we believe Him to be the Son of God and place our trust in Him, we are loosed from our sin. Our hearts are cleansed from sin. We become children of God by faith in His risen Son. And we are free to serve Him.

Paul was a child of God. Timothy was a child of God. Are *you* a child of God? If you are, you have a message to tell others.

2. A SERVANT OF GOD MUST BE YIELDED TO GOD

If you want to serve God, you must be yielded to Him. To yield to Him is to give yourself completely to Him. In this series of lessons we have learned an important verse. Shall we say it together? "I beseech you therefore, brethren, by the mercies of God, that you present your bodies a living sacrifice, holy, acceptable unto God, which is your reasonable service" (Romans 12:1). This means that God wants every part of you so you can witness for Jesus Christ.

Show Illustration #14a

He wants your entire body. He wants your mind. He wants you to allow Him to control your thoughts. He wants your ears and eyes.

– 25 –

Show Illustration #14b

He wants your hands and feet–feet which will go where He wants you to go.

Show Illustration #14c

He wants your mouth–a mouth which He can fill with messages of Himself.

If you do not give yourself completely to God, you will give yourself to sin. (See Romans 6:11-23.) John Mark turned back from serving God. And, although he repented and was later willing to serve, he was refused the privilege of working with the greatest of all missionaries, the Apostle Paul.

Suppose you were hired to drive a bus. (*Teacher:* Mention the kind of transportation your people know–jeepney, lorry, truck, camel, train, boat.) After being hired you say to your employer, "I am glad to work for you. But there is one thing you must be told: I shall drive your bus, but I shall take it where *I* want to take it." How long do you think you would drive the bus?

If you are a child of God by faith in His Son, then your body belongs to God. Are you willing to let God use your feet to take you anywhere He wants you to go? To Africa, India, South America or to your neighbors and friends? Will you let God use your hands to help others, as Jason did? Are you willing for God to use your mouth–saying whatever He wants you to say? Will you allow God to control your eyes so you will not look at anything He disapproves? Will you let God control your mind? This is what it means to be a living sacrifice to God. Is your body such a sacrifice?

As we have seen, a servant of God is, first of all, a *blood-bought child of God*. A servant of God must be *yielded* to God. Now let me ask you a question: Do you think God deserves the very best? Of course He does. This next section then is extremely important.

3. GOD WANTS HIS SERVANTS TO BE PREPARED AND TRAINED

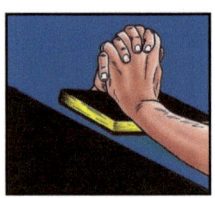

Show Illustration #15a

God wants prepared servants.

The Apostle Paul was a well-trained man, even before he was saved. After he received Jesus Christ as his Saviour, he realized there was much more he needed to know. This is why he went to the desert. There he studied the Word of God. Through that study the Lord spoke to Paul.

Show Illustration #15b

Because Paul knew the Lord God, he talked to Him in prayer. As a result of those years of study and prayer, Paul became a famous worldwide missionary.

If a man is going to be a doctor, he gives many years of his life studying how to be a doctor. A teacher studies for a long time in order to teach. Surely, then, God's work requires training and preparation. By carefully studying the Word of God, you can learn how to be a good servant of God. (See 2 Timothy 2:15; 3:15-16; Romans 10:17.) Your training will not be complete unless you also add prayer to Bible study. (See James 1:5.) Talk to God and let God talk to you.

You prepare yourself for Christian service by reading God's Word and praying in your own quiet time each day. You can be prepared in church, in Bible study groups, in a Bible school or college, or through Bible correspondence courses.

Learn as much as you can as well as you can and as soon as you can. Do not wait until you are old. If you cannot go to a Bible school or seminary, start studying the Bible by yourself, and in church and Sunday school.

Write these truths in your notebook:

To be a servant of God

1. I must be *converted*.

    Paul, Silas, Barnabas, Timothy were converted. They trusted in the Lord Jesus and turned to God from their sin. This new life should make me want to serve God.
2. I must be *yielded* to God and willing to obey Him.
3. I should be *trained* and *prepared for service*.
4. *Service for God begins now*.

4. TRUE SERVICE FOR GOD BEGINS NOW

Paul started witnessing for God immediately after his conversion–even before he studied and prepared to serve. He told others about Jesus Christ, the Son of God. He told them about the death and resurrection of Jesus. You can share this with others. As you serve, you will be training and preparing yourself to be a better servant. People everywhere are lost. They must hear the Gospel. Will they hear it from *you*?

Perhaps you wonder exactly how you can witness to others.

Show Back Page Cover

(*Teacher:* If you have a Wordless Book, you may prefer to use it.)

You can witness of your faith in Christ by using colors, saying: This black reminds us of night when it is dark. Men rob houses and commit other sins when it is dark. Once I was in darkness of sin. I did wrong because I was a sinner. (See John 3:18-19.)

Then I learned that the Lord Jesus Christ, the Son of God came from Heaven to earth. He is absolutely perfect and never did or said or thought anything wrong. One day He died and gave His precious blood. (Point to the red.) When He died on the cross, He took the punishment I deserve for my sins. (See Isaiah 53:6; 1 Peter 2:24.)

But the Lord Jesus did not stay dead. He proved He is the Son of God by rising from the dead. I believe Him to be the Son of God and have placed my trust in Him. I have asked His forgiveness. (Point to white and to empty tomb.) So my sins are forgiven. (See 1 Corinthians 15:3-4.)

Now I have His kind of life–everlasting life. And I shall live forever with Him in beautiful Heaven (point to gold) where even the street is gold. (See John 3:16; Revelation 3:20; 21:21.)

I am a servant of the living God and of His Son, the Lord Jesus. I want to tell you that even though you are a sinner, you too can have everlasting life. If you believe that the Lord Jesus is the Son of God, if you are willing to place your trust in Him and turn from your sin, you will receive His kind of life–everlasting life. Someday you will be with Him forever in His home, Heaven.

This is one way to tell others what you know. Will you, like Paul, be a servant of Jesus Christ?

Maybe you are wondering: *Where should I witness?* As God led Paul in the long ago, so He will lead you. By spending time with God, He will place in your mind the name of the place He wants you to go with His message.

Perhaps you say: *What shall I do if I am placed in jail for witnessing?* Like Paul, you may suffer for your witness. But God will be with you every moment.

Suppose they threaten to take my life? you ask. Many have given their lives for the sake of Christ. You cannot know beforehand whether God will help you escape (as He helped Paul to escape often) or if you will die (as Stephen did). No matter what comes, you may be sure God will remember you have given yourself to Him as a living sacrifice. And one day He will reward you for your service.

Will you present your body to Him today for whatever He wants?

www.ingramcontent.com/pod-product-compliance
Lightning Source LLC
Chambersburg PA
CBHW060805090426
42736CB00002B/163